W

A Benjamin Blog
and his Inquisitive Dog
Guide

Republic of Ireland

Anita Ganeri

heinemann
raintree

Edited by Helen Cox Cannons and Tony Wacholtz
Designed by Steve Mead
Original illustrations © Capstone Global Library
   Limited 2015
Illustrated by Sernur ISIK
Picture research by Svetlana Zhurkin
Production by Helen McCreath
Originated by Capstone Global Library Limited
Printed and bound in China by CTPS

18 17 16 15 14
10 9 8 7 6 5 4 3 2 1

Library of Congress Cataloging-in-Publication Data

Ganeri, Anita, 1961-
  Ireland / Anita Ganeri.
    pages cm.—(Country guides, with Benjamin Blog and his inquisitive dog)
Includes bibliographical references and index.
ISBN 978-1-4109-6849-4 (hb)—ISBN 978-1-4109-6857-9 (pb)—ISBN 978-1-4109-6872-2 (ebook) 1. Ireland—Juvenile literature. I. Title.
  DA906.G37 2015
  941.7—dc23   2014013379

Acknowledgments

We would like to thank the following for permission to reproduce photographs: Alamy: Mikel Bilbao Gorostiaga Travels, 6; Dreamstime: Fr3ank33, 12; iStockphotos: martinturzak, 20, sharynos, 14; Newscom: Arco Images G/picture alliance/W. Dieterich, 7, Danita Delimont Photography/William Sutton, 25, Design Pics/George Munday, 8, Design Pics/The Irish Image Collection, 26, Robert Harding/Jeremy Lightfoot, 23, World History Archive, 27, 29; Shutterstock: Andrei Nekrassov, 13, Andres Ello, 9, AridOcean, 5, Eoghan McNally, 22, Javier Soto Vazquez, 11, Martina I. Meyer, 24, MShev, 21, Patryk Kosmider, 18, Paul Stringer, 28, Peter Fuchs, cover, SandyS, 19, Stuart Monk, 15, Thierry Maffeis, 17, Wesley Cowpar, 10; Stockbyte, 4; SuperStock: Hemis.fr, 16.

Every effort has been made to contact copyright holders of material reproduced in this book. Any omissions will be rectified in subsequent printings if notice is given to the publisher.

Some words are shown in bold, **like this.** You can find out what they mean by looking in the glossary.

Contents

Welcome to the Republic of Ireland!

Hello! My name is Benjamin Blog, and this is Barko Polo, my **inquisitive** dog. (He's named after the ancient explorer **Marco Polo**.) We have just returned from our latest adventure—exploring the Republic of Ireland. We put this book together from some of the blog posts we wrote on the way.

NORTHERN IRELAND

REPUBLIC OF IRELAND

Dublin

Limerick

Cork

BARKO'S BLOG-TASTIC IRELAND FACTS

Ireland is an island in the Atlantic Ocean, off the west coast of Great Britain. The northeast corner of the island is called Northern Ireland and is part of the United Kingdom. The rest of the island is called the Republic of Ireland.

Story of Ireland

Posted by: Ben Blog | December 21 at noon

Our first stop in Ireland was Newgrange, an amazing **tomb** built more than 5,000 years ago. It was carefully designed so that, on the shortest day of the year (that's today), the sun shines through a hole above the door straight into the main burial chamber. What a sight!

BARKO'S BLOG-TASTIC IRELAND FACTS

From 1845 to 1851, a **famine** struck Ireland. A disease killed the potato crop that many people relied on for food. Around a million people died, and millions more left Ireland. This statue in Dublin remembers that terrible time.

Coasts, Cliffs, and Mountains

Posted by: Ben Blog | January 10 at 1:56 p.m.

We're now on the Blasket Islands, off the southwest coast of Ireland. The wind is very strong here. People used to live on these islands but, with no electricity or running water, life was very tough. In 1953, the last islanders moved to the **mainland**, leaving their homes behind.

BARKO'S BLOG-TASTIC IRELAND FACTS

Peat bogs cover large parts of Ireland. They are home to lots of different plants, such as sphagnum moss, bog rosemary, and sundews, like these beauties, which trap insects to eat.

Staying in the west of Ireland, I set off to climb Carrauntoohil. At 3,406 feet (1,038 meters) tall, it is the highest mountain in Ireland and is part of a mountain range called Macgillycuddy's Reeks. It is a bit of a trek up to the big metal cross that marks the top.

BARKO'S BLOG-TASTIC IRELAND FACTS
This is the Burren, a huge, rocky area in County Clare. It is crisscrossed by deep, jagged cracks. These are called grykes and are made by water wearing the rock away.

City Streets

Posted by: Ben Blog | February 9 at 6:45 p.m.

From Carrauntoohil, we headed east to Dublin. It is the biggest city in Ireland and the capital city. Barko took this snapshot of O'Connell Bridge, which crosses the Liffey River. The river flows through the center of the city. We're off to Dublin Castle next.

BARKO'S BLOG-TASTIC IRELAND FACTS

Ireland's second-largest city is Cork, in the south. This is the old Cork City Gaol (say "jail"). You can visit a cell and see what life was like for criminals in the 1800s.

Dia duit!

Posted by: Ben Blog | March 1 at 10:01 a.m.

About 4.6 million people live in Ireland. Most people speak English, but some people also speak Irish. In Irish, *Dia duit* means "hello." Irish is mostly spoken in the west, and children have to learn it in school. There are also Irish-language stations on TV and the radio.

BARKO'S BLOG-TASTIC IRELAND FACTS

Over the last 175 years, many people have left Ireland to live and work in other countries such as England, the United States, and Canada. They have taken their Irish traditions with them.

In Ireland, most children start school when they are five years old. Most schools teach the children in English, but some schools teach them in Irish. In some places, schools are very small. One school on the island of Inishturk has only two teachers and seven students.

BARKO'S BLOG-TASTIC IRELAND FACTS

Some students go on to college after high school. This is Trinity College, in the middle of Dublin. It is the oldest university in Ireland and has around 17,000 students.

It is St. Patrick's Day—the biggest celebration in Ireland. We're here in Limerick, with a huge crowd, to watch the grand parade. St. Patrick is the patron saint of Ireland. Legend says that he was captured by pirates and brought to Ireland as a slave when he was 16 years old.

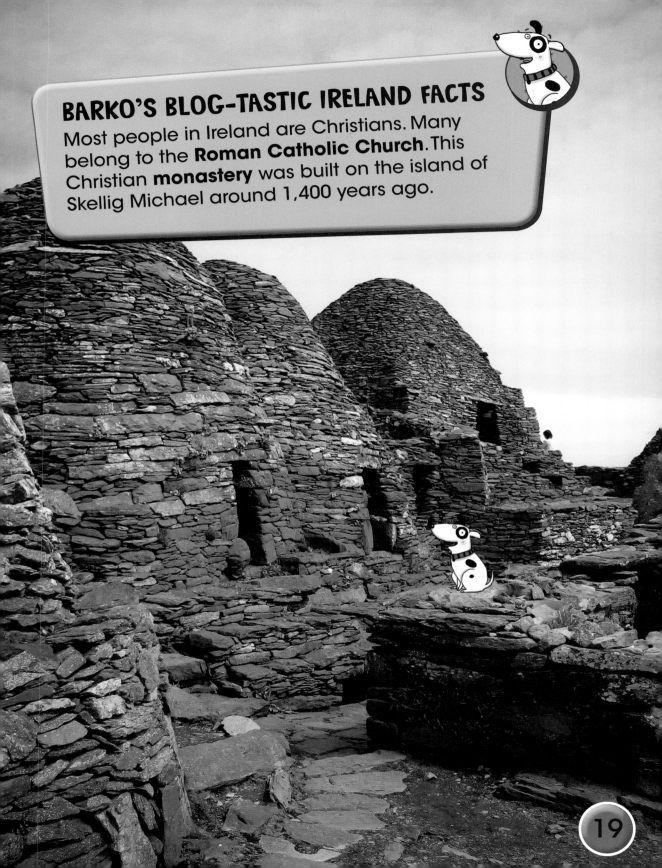

Most people in Ireland are Christians. Many belong to the **Roman Catholic Church**. This Christian **monastery** was built on the island of Skellig Michael around 1,400 years ago.

Time for Dinner...

After a long, tiring day, we were hungry, so we stopped off for some food. I wanted something filling, so I had a big bowl of Irish stew. It is a stew made from lamb, potatoes, carrots, onions, and parsley. It was very tasty, but I couldn't eat another mouthful.

20

BARKO'S BLOG-TASTIC IRELAND FACTS

Barmbrack is sweet bread with raisins. On Halloween, things are hidden inside, such as a coin and a ring. If you get a slice with the coin, it means that you are going to be rich!

Good *Craic*

Posted by: Ben Blog | August 18 at 3:30 p.m.

Back in Dublin, we're at Croke Park to watch a Gaelic football match. Gaelic football is the most popular sport in Ireland. It is a bit like a blend of soccer and football. Players can kick, bounce, or throw the ball. The match is so noisy!

BARKO'S BLOG-TASTIC IRELAND FACTS

This band is playing traditional Irish music. Irish musicians often play **fiddles**, whistles, and drums. The music is lively and catchy, and you can't help singing and dancing along.

From Cows to Crystal

Posted by: Ben Blog | October 2 at 3:34 p.m.

Ireland has rich soil and lots of rain, which means that grass grows well. Animals such as cows and sheep graze on the grass. Cows are raised for their meat and milk. The milk is also turned into butter and cheese. Farmers also grow crops such as wheat, oats, and **sugar beet**.

K2 - 12

BARKO'S BLOG-TASTIC IRELAND FACTS

The city of Waterford in southeast Ireland is famous for making a special kind of glass called crystal. The glass is blown into shapes and used to make vases, glasses, clocks, and even **chandeliers**.

And Finally...

Our last stop was Blarney Castle, near Cork. At the top of one of its towers is a block of stone called the Blarney Stone. Legend says that if you kiss the stone, you will get the **gift of the gab**. But you have to hang upside down over the **battlements** to reach the stone. Yikes!

BARKO'S BLOG-TASTIC IRELAND FACTS

The Book of Kells in Trinity College, Dublin, was written by Christian **monks** around 1,300 years ago. It contains part of the Bible and is illustrated with beautiful pictures. It is one of Ireland's most precious treasures.

Ireland Fact File

Area: 27,133 square miles
(70,273 square kilometers)

Population: 4,832,765 (2014)

Capital city: Dublin

Other main cities: Cork, Galway, Limerick

Languages: English, Irish

Main religion: Roman Catholicism

Highest mountain: Carrauntoohil
(3,415 feet/1,041 meters)

Longest river: Shannon (240 miles/386 kilometers)

Currency: Euro

Ireland Quiz

Find out how much you know about Ireland with our quick quiz.

1. Which is the highest mountain in Ireland?
a) Ben Nevis
b) Scafell Pike
c) Carrauntoohil

2. Which river flows through Dublin?
a) Shannon
b) Liffey
c) Bann

3. What does *Dia duit* mean?
a) hello
b) goodbye
c) how are you?

4. When is St. Patrick's Day?
a) March 16
b) March 18
c) March 17

5. What is this?

5. the Book of Kells
4. c
3. a
2. b
1. c
Answers

29

Glossary

battlement stepped wall around the top of a castle

chandelier decorative light fixture that hangs down from the ceiling

craic Irish word for having a good time and talking with friends

famine time when people starve to death because there is not enough food

fiddle another name for a violin

gift of the gab able to speak well and cleverly

inquisitive interested in learning about the world

mainland main part of a landmass

Marco Polo explorer who lived from about 1254 to 1324. He traveled from Italy to China.

monastery place where monks live and worship

monk man who devotes his life to worshipping god

peat material found in the ground that is mainly made of rotting plants

Roman Catholic Church part of the Christian Church

sugar beet plant with roots that are used to produce sugar

tomb place where dead bodies are buried

Find Out More

Books

Blashfield, Jean F. *Ireland* (Enchantment of the World). New York: Children's Press, 2014.

McQuinn, Anna, and Colm McQuinn. *Ireland* (Countries of the World). Washington, D.C.: National Geographic, 2008.

Waldron, Melanie. *Ireland* (Countries Around the World). Chicago: Heinemann Library, 2012.

Web sites

Facthound offers a safe, fun way to find Internet sites related to this book. All of the sites on Facthound have been researched by our staff.

Here's all you do:

Visit *www.facthound.com*

Type in this code: 9781410968494

Index